A Sh[...]
Cornish Dictionary

Gerlyver Ber

Christine Truran

DYLLANSOW TRURAN

First published 1986

Dyllansow Truran
Cornish Publications
Trewolsta, Trewirgie, Redruth, Cornwall

Copyright © 1986 Christine Truran

Prepared for publication and typeset by
St Day Computer Services
Burnwithian Terrace, St Day, Redruth

Printed and bound in Great Britain by
Short Run Press Ltd., Exeter

ISBN 1 85022 015 8

FOREWORD

This Shorter Cornish Dictionary has been produced for the learners who feel the need for something more easy to use than the larger dictionary and its supplements. The vocabulary is tailored to suit the needs of students in the early stages of learning.

It is also meant to cater for the needs of the casual enquirer and to serve as a handy reference book for anyone needing to have some elementary knowledge of Cornish. A list of further reference books in and around the language can be found after page 60.

I would like to thank in particular Rod Lyon for his help in the preparation of this book and Paul Johns for his professional advice and encouragement.

Among the peculiarities of Cornish are its mutations - the system whereby some words alter the first letter of the following word or words. For example, **tas** means "father" - but you are likely to come across **dha das**, "your father", or **ow thas**, "my father". There's no need for panic! Even before you've fully learnt the mutation system, you can find your way around it by means of the table of mutations. Column 1 gives the original first letter of the word - the one it's listed under in the dictionary. Columns 2, 3, 4 and 5 give the different mutations. Suppose you want to find out what **dha das** means. When you look up **dha,** you'll find that it has a figure 2 after it - **dha²**. The 2 refers to column 2 of the mutation table. All you have to do is to find 'd' in column 2; find out that the original letter was 't', from column 1; and then look up **tas**.

TABLE OF MUTATIONS

1	2	3	4	5
b	v	b	p	f,v
c,k	h	h	c	c
ch	j	ch	ch	ch
d	dh	d	t	t
g	-,w	g	c,k	h
gw	w	gw	qu	wh
m	v	m	m	f,v
p	b	f	p	p
qu	gw	wh	qu	qu
t	d	th	t	t

ABBREVIATIONS USED

adj.	adjective	f.	feminine	pl.	plural
col.	collective	m.	masculine	v.	verb

a²	verbal particle
a²	from, of
a brys ysel	cheap
a drus	across
a ugh	above
abarth	for, on the part of
acont, m	account
adal	opposite
adermyn	on time
adhelergh	behind
adherak	in front of
adhesempys	suddenly
adhyworth	from
adro	around, about
adryf dhe	behind
aga³	their
agan	our
agas	your (plural)
agensow	recently
ages	than
ahes	along
Alban, f	Scotland
als, f, alsyow	cliff
alwheth, m, alwhethow	key
amal, m, emlow	edge, side
amanyn, m	butter
amary, m, amarys	cupboard
ambosa, v	promise
ameth, f	agriculture
amser, f, amserow	time
an	the
an lacca	worst
ankevy, v	forget
anwos, m	cold
apern, m, apronyow	apron
arak	in front of

aral,(erel,pl)	other
aral	another
arghans	money
arghanty,m,arghantyow	bank
arta	again
asclas,col	chips
asclatty,m,asclattyow	chipshop
asclejen,f,asclas	chip
ascorn,m,eskern	bone
askel,f,eskelly	wing
assaya,v	try
aswon,v	know (recognise)
atalgyst,f,atalgystyow	dustbin
athves	ripe
aval,m,avallow	apple
avar	early
avel	like
aves	outside
avon,f,avenow	river
avorow	tomorrow
awartha	above
awoles	below
awos	because
ayren,f,ayrennow	aeroplane
baban,m/f,babanas	baby
badhya,v	bathe
bagas,m,bagasow	group,team
bakken,m	bacon
bal,m,balow	mine
baner,m,banerow	flag
bara,m	bread
bardhes,f,bardhesow	bard (female)
barf,f,barvow	beard
bargen tyr,m	farm
barth,m,byrth	bard (male)
bason,m,basonnow	basin

bat,m,battys	bat (cricket)
bath,m,bathow	coin
bedha,v	dare
benen,f,benenes	woman
ber,adj	short
bera,v	drop
beth,m,bedhow	grave
bew	alive,lively
bewnans,m,bewnansow	life
blas,m	taste,smell
bledhen,f,bledhynnow	year
blejen,f,blejennow	flower
bles,m	flour
blewen,f,blew	hair
bloth,m	years,age
bodhar,adj	deaf
bogh,f,dywvogh	cheek
boghosek,adj	poor
bolla,m,bollow	bowl
bolunjeth,m	wish
bonk,m,bonkys	bump
bos,v	be
bos,m	food
bos,m	bush
bosty,m,bostyow	restaurant
bottel,m,bottellow	bottle
bownder,f,bownderyow	lane
braf,adj	fine,splendid
bran,f,bryny	crow
bras	big
bre,f,breow	hill
bregh,f,dywvregh	arm
bresel,m/f,breselow	war
Breten Vyghan,f	Brittany
Breten Vur,f	Britain
Bretennek	British
Breton,m,Bretonyon	Breton (male)

Bretones,f,Bretonyon	Breton (female)
brewyonen,brewyon	crumb
bro,f,broyow	country
broder,m,breder	brother
bryn,m,brynnow	hill
budhy,v	drown
bugh,f,bughas	cow
bus,m,bussow	bus
busaf,m,busavow	bus-stop
bush,m,bushys	crowd
byghan	small
bys,m	world
bys	until
bys,m,besyas	finger
bys vyken	for ever
bysow,m,besewow	ring
bysy	busy
byth	ever
bythqueth	ever
cadar,f,caderyow	chair
cadar vreghek,f	armchair
caderyer,m,caderyoryon	chairman
cafas,m,cafasow	can (container)
cafasa,v	can
cafos,v	find
cafos,v	have,get
cales	difficult,hard
caltor,f,caltoryow	kettle
cam,m,cammow	step
cam,adj	wrong,crooked
can,f,cannow	song
cana,v	sing,play instrument
canker,m,kencras	crab
cans,m,cansow	hundred
canstel,f,canstellow	basket
car,m,kerry	car

car,m,kerens	friend
cara,v	love
caretysen,f,caretys	carrot
carjy,m,carjyow	garage
carrek,f,carrygy	rock
carten,f,cartennow	card
carten-post,f,cartennow-post	post-card
cas,adj	hateful
cath,f,cathas	cat
cawlen,f,cawl	cabbage
chambour,m,chambours	bedroom
chy,m,chyow	house
chy byghan,m,chyow byghan	lavatory
chymbla,m	chimney
claf,adj	ill,sick
clafcar,m,clafkerry	ambulance
clavjy,m,clavjyow	hospital
clavyjores,f,clavyjoresow	nurse
cleth	north,left
clewes,v	hear,smell
clok,m	clock
cloppek,adj	lame
cober,m	copper
codha,v	fall
coffy,m	coffee
cofhe,v	remember
coger,m,cogeryow	cooker
cok,m,cucow	fishing boat
cola orth,v	lend
collel,f,kellyl	knife
collenky,v	swallow
comolen,f,comol	cloud
con,f	supper
conna,m	neck
connek,adj	clever
consel,m	council
consler,m	councillor

convedhes,v	understand
conyn,m,conynas	rabbit
coref,m	beer
corf,m,corfow	body
cosel,adj	quiet
cost,m,costys	cost
coth,adj	old
cowal,adj	whole
coweth,m,cowetha	friend
cowethas,f,cowethasow	society
cowl,m	soup
coynt,adj	strange
cras,col	toast
cref,adj	strong
cregy,v	hang
cren,adj	round
crenna,v	shake
cres,m,cresow	middle
cres,m	centre (circle)
cresen,f	centre (health...)
cresyk,cresygow	crisp (potato)
croghen,f	skin
croglen,f	curtain
crow,m,crowyow	shed
crowshensy	crossroads
crowst,m,crowstys	lunch (picnic)
crya,v	cry
cryb,f,crybow	comb
crys,m,crysyow	shirt
crysy,v	believe
cudha,v	hide
cuf,adj	kind,dear
cul,adj	narrow
cun,m	dogs
cusca,v	sleep
cyder,m	cider
cygaret,m,cygaretys	cigarette

da,adj	good
dall,adj	blind
dalleth,m	start
dalleth,v	begin
damawyn,f,dammyow gwyn	granny
dans,m,dyns	tooth
danvon,v	send
darn,m,darnow	bit,small piece
darras,m,darrajow	door
davas,f,deves	sheep
de,m	yesterday
de Gwener	Friday
de Lun	Monday
de Mergher	Wednesday
de Merth	Tuesday
de Sadorn	Saturday
de Sul	Sunday
de Yow	Thursday
dedhewy,v	promise
degea,v	shut,close
degensete,m	day before yesterday
degensow	recently
degol,m,degolyow	holiday
dehen,m	cream
dehen rewys,m	ice cream
dek	ten
del	as
delen,f,del,delkyow	leaf
delynya,v	draw
demedhyans,m,demedhyansow	wedding
den,m,tus	man
deneren,f,denerennow	penny
deryvas,v	tell,announce
desempys,adj	sudden
desmygy,v	guess,invent
deth,m,dedhyow	day
deu^2,m	two

deudhek	twelve
devera,v	pour
Dew genes	goodbye
Dew	God
dewas,f,dewosow	drink
dewedha,v	end
dewedhes	late
deweth,m	end
dewheles,v	return
Dewnans,f	Devon
dewotty,m,dewottyow	pub
dewys,v	choose
dha^2	your (singular)
dhe^2	to
dhe les,adj	useful
dohajeth	afternoon
don,v	carry
donsya,v	dance
dorn,m,deudhorn	hand,fist
dos,v	arrive,come
down,adj	deep
dowr,m,dowrow	water
dowst,m	dust
dre^2	through
drehevel,v	build,lift
dres	past,over
drok,adj	bad
droklam,m,droklammow	accident
dry,v	bring
du,adj	black
Du,m	November
dybry,v	eat
dyek,adj	lazy
dyeskynna,v	come down
dyfuna,v	wake up
dyghow,m	south,right
dyllajow	clothes

dyllas,m,dyllajow	item of clothing
dyndyl,v	earn
dynsel,v	bite,chew
dynsor,m,dynsoryon	dentist
dyogel,adj	safe,certain
dyscajor,m,dyscajoryon	teacher
dyscajores,f,dyscajoresow	teacher
dyscas,m,dyscasow	lesson
dysky,v	learn
dysquedhes,v	show
dystough	immediately
dystrewy,v	destroy
dyw^2,f	two
dyworth	from
dywros,f,dywrosow	bicycle
dywwyth	twice
dywysygneth,m	industry
ebren,f	sky
edhen,f,ydhyn	bird
edrek,m	regret
ef	he,it (m)
efan,adj	wide
eglos,f,eglosyow	church
elgeth,f,elgethyow	chin
elyn,m,deuelyn	elbow
ena	there
enclathva,f	cemetery
enep,m,enebow	face
eneval,m,enevelas	animal
ensompel,m,ensomplys	example
entra,v	enter
enys,f,enesow	island
er,adj	fresh
erbyn	against
erel	others
ergh,m	snow

erghy,v	order
erna²	until
ervyra,v	decide
es	than
es,adj	easy
esedha,v	sit
eseth,f,esedhow	seat
esethva,f,esethvaow	sitting-room
eskys,f,skyjyow	shoe
estren,m,estrenyon	stranger
estyllen,f,estyllenow	shelf
etek,adj	eighteen
eth,adj	eight
ethom,m	need
eva,v	drink
ewl bos,f	appetite
ewn,adj	correct
ewna,v	mend,correct
ewnter,m,ewntras	uncle
ewyn,m,ewynas	fingernail,claw
fardel,m,fardellow	bundle,luggage
fatel	how
faven,f,faf	bean
fenester,f,fenestry	window
fenten,f,fentynyow	well
fetha,v	beat
flogh,m,fleghes	child
floghwyn,m,fleghes gwyn	grandchild
flows,m	rubbish (verbal)
fol,adj	foolish
folen,f,folennow	page
forgh,f,fergh	fork
forn,f,fornow	oven
forth,f,fordhow	road,way
forth-horn,f,fordhow-horn	railway
fos,f,fosow	wall

frut,m,frutys	fruit
frya,v	fry
Frynk,f	France
fur,adj	wise
furf,f,furvyow	shape
fusyk,adj	lucky
fyllel,v	fail
fystyna,v	hurry
fyt,m,fyttys	match (game)
galar,m	pain,grief
gallos,v	be able
gallosek,adj	powerful
ganow,m,ganowow	mouth
gans	with
gar,f,dywar	leg
garma,v	shout
garow,adj	rough
gasa,v	leave
gava,v	forgive
gavar,f,gever	goat
gell,adj	brown
gelwel,v	invite,name,call
Genver,m	January
genys	born
ger,m,geryow	word
gerlyver,m,gerlyfrow	dictionary
glan,adj	clean
glanhe,v	clean
glas,adj	blue
glaw,m	rain
glena orth,v	stick
glow,col	coal (fuel)
glus,m	glue
glyn,m,deulyn	knee
glyn,m,glynnow	valley (dry)
glyp,adj	wet

gober,m,gobrow	pay
goky,adj	stupid
golghy,v	wash (not oneself)
golow,m,golowys	light
gon,m,gonnys	gun
gorfenna,v	finish
gorhel,m,gorholyon	ship
gorhemmyn,v	order
gorher,m,gorheryow	lid
gorra,v	put
gorsaf,m,gorsavow	station
gortheby,v	reply
Gortheren,m	July
gorthewer,m	evening
gorthyp,m	answer
gortos,v	wait
gos,m	blood
goslowes,v	listen
gothvos,v	know,understand
gour,m	husband
govyn,v	ask
growetha,v	lie down
grysys	stairs
gul,v	do,make
Gwaf,m,Gwavow	winter
gwak,adj	empty
gwan,adj	weak
gwandra,v	wander
gwartha,m	top
gwarthek,col	cattle
gwary,v	play
gwary,m	game
gwasca,v	squeeze
gwaya,v	move
gwaynya,v	win
Gwaynten,v	spring
gwaytya,v	hope

gweder,m,gwedrow	glass (material)
gweder myras,m	mirror
gwedhen,f,gwyth	tree
gwedren,f,gwedrennow	glass (drinking)
gweles,v	see
gwell,adj	better
gwella,adj	best
gwellhe,v	improve
gwelsow byghan,m	scissors
gwely,m,gwelyow	bed
gwer,adj	green
gweres,v	help
gwerth,f	sale
gwertha,v	sell
gwerthjy,m,gwerthjyow	shop
gweth,adj	worse
gwetha,adj	worst
gwlan,col	wool
gwlas,f,gwlasow	country
gwrynya,v	wrestle
gwrek,f,gwrageth	wife
gwyn,m	wine
gwyn,adj	white
gwyns,m,gwynsow	wind
gwyr,adj	true
gwysca,v	wear,dress
gwythva,f	factory
gwythyades,f,gwythyadesow	policewoman
gwythyas,m,gwythysy	policeman
ha	and
Haf,m,Havow	summer
hag	and
hager,adj	ugly
hager awel,f	storm
hanaf,m,hanavow	cup
haneth	tonight

hanow,m,hynwyn	name
hansel,m,hansellow	breakfast
hanter	half
hartha,v	bark
heb	without
hedhy,v	stop
hedhyu	today
hedra	while
Hedra,m	October
hel,m,helow	hall
hem	this
hembronk,v	lead
hemma,m	this,this one
hen	that
hen,adj	old (former)
henna,m	that one,that
hep	without
hep cost	free (without cost)
hes,m	length
hevelep	like
hogh,m,mogh	pig
holan,m	salt
hom	this
homma,f	this one,this
hon	that
honen	self
honna,f	that one,that
hos,m,heyjy	duck
hot,m	hat
howl,m	sun
howldrehevel,m	east
howlsedhas,m	west
hunros,m	dream
hy,f	she,her,it
hyr,adj	long

jawl,m	devil
junnya,v	join
ke,m,keow	hedge
kegy,v	cook
kegyn,f,kegynow	kitchen
kekefrys	also
kelly,v	lose
kelmy,v	tie
kelorn,m	bucket
Kembrek	Welsh
Kembres,f,Kembresow	Welshwoman
Kembro,m,Kembryon	Welshman
Kembry	Wales
kemeres,v	take
kemmys	as much
kempen,adj	tidy
kempoller,m	computer
kemysk,m	mixture
kenderow,m,kendrywy	cousin
kenethel,f,kenethlow	nation
kens	before
kensa	first
kentevyn,m	concrete
kenytherow,f,kenythrywy	cousin
kepar	like
ker	dear
kerdhes,v	walk
kerens,m	friends,parents
kerghes,v	fetch
Kernewek,adj	Cornish
Kernewes,f,Kernewesow	Cornishwoman
Kernow,m,Kernowyon	Cornishman
Kernow,f	Cornwall
kerry,pl	cars
kert,m,kertys	lorry
kes,m	cheese

keskelm,m	cement
kettel	as soon as
kevranna,v	share
kewar,adj	accurate
kewer,f	weather
kewerder,m	accuracy
kewsel,v	talk,speak
keyn,m,keynow	back
ky,m,cun	dog
kyfvewy,m	party (birthday..)
kyfyth,m	jam
kyger,m	butcher
kyk,m	meat
kyk bowyn,m	beef
kyk mogh,m	pork
kyn⁵	although
Kynyaf,m	autumn
kynyow,m,kynyewyow	dinner (midday)
kyst,f,kystyow	box
kyttryn,m,kyttrynyow	bus
lacca,adj	worse
lader,m,ladron	thief
ladha,v	kill
ladra,v	steal
lagas,m,deulagas	eye
lagha,m,laghys	law
lamma,v	jump
lavrak,m,lavregow	trousers
le,m,leow	place
le	less
ledan,adj	wide
leder,f,ledrow	slope
lef,m,levow	voice
lemmyn	now
len,f,lennow	cloth
lenky,v	swallow

lent,adj	slow
lenwel,v	fill
les,m	width
lesky,v	burn
leth,m	milk
leverel,v	say,tell
lewyas,v	drive (a car)
lo,f,loyow	spoon
lor,f	moon
los,adj	grey
losowen,f,losow	vegetable
lost,m,lostow	tail
losten,f,lostennow	skirt
Loundres,f	London
lovan,f,lovonnow	rope
lowarth,f,lowarthow	garden
lowen,adj	happy
lowr,adj	enough
luf,f,dywluf	hand
lughes,col	lightning
lun,adj	full
lur,m,luryow	floor,ground
lusow,f	ashes
lyes,adj	many
lyha	least
lym,adj	sharp
lyn,f,lynnow	lake
lyther,m,lytheryow	letter
lytherwas,m,lytherwesyon	postman
lyver,m,lyfrow	book
lyverjy,m,lyverjyow	library (building)
lyverva,f	library (of books)
lyw,m,lywyow	colour
lywyans,m,lywyansow	picture
-ma	this
mam,f,mammow	mother

manek,f,manegow	glove
map,m,mebyon	son
mappa,m,mappys	map
mar⁴	if
mar²	so
mar plek	please
margh,m,mergh	horse
marghas,f,marghasow	market
marnas	unless
marner,m,marners	sailor
marow,adj	dead
martesen	perhaps
marth,m	surprise
marthys,adj	wonderful
maw,m,mebyon	boy
may,mayth,⁵	that,so that,where
may,mayth,⁵	where (relative)
maylyer,m	envelope
Me,m	May
mebyl,col	furniture
medheges,f,medhegesow	doctor
medhek,m,medhygyon	doctor
medhekneth,m	medicine
medhel,adj	soft
medhow,adj	drunk
megy,v	smoke
mel,m	honey
melen,adj	yellow
melyn,f,melynyow	mill
men,m,meyn	stone
meneth,m,menythyow	hill
menough	often
Merth,m	March
merwel,v	die
mes	but,out
mes,m,mesyow	field (large,open)
mesva,f,mesvedhy	inch

meth,f	shame
Metheven,m	June
modryp,f,modrebeth	aunt
mogh,pl	pigs
mollethy,v	swear,curse
mon,adj	slim
mor,m,morow	sea
moren,f,mor	blackberry
morthol,m,mortholow	hammer
mos,f,mosow	table
mos,v	go
mowes,f,mowysy	girl
moy	more
moyha	most
mur,adj	great
mur ras	thanks
myghtern,m,myghterneth	king
myghternes,f,myghternesow	queen
myl,f,mylyow	thousand
myl,m,mylas	animal
myldyr,m,myldyryow	mile
mylva,f,mylvaow	zoo
mynnes,v	want
mynysen,f,mynysennow	minute
myras orth,v	look
myrgh,f,myrghes	daughter
mys,m,mysyow	month
mys Du,m	November
mys Ebrel,m	April
mys Est,m	August
mys Genver,m	January
mys Gortheren,m	July
mys Gwyngala,m	September
mys Hedra,m	October
mys Kevardhu,m	December
mys Me,m	May
mys Merth,m	March

mys Metheven,m	June
mys Whevrer,m	February
myttyn,m,myttynow	morning
-na	that
na	nor,not
Nadelek,m	Christmas
nag	nor,not
nagha,v	refuse,deny
namna^2	almost
namoy	no more
nans,m,nansow	valley
naw	nine
nawnjek	nineteen
nebes	some,few
nebonen	someone
nefra	never
negys,m,negysyow	message,business
nen,m,nennow	ceiling
nep	who (relative)
neppyth	something
nerth,m	strength
nes	closer
nessa	nearest,next
nessa,v	approach
newl,m	fog
newodhow	news
nor,m	world
nos,f,nosow	night
noswyth	at night,night-time
noweth,adj	new
nown,m	hunger
noy,m,noyens	nephew
nuvya,v	swim
ny^2	not
ny	we
nyhewer	night (last)

nyja,v	fly
nyth,m	nest
nyver,m,nyverow	number
nyvera,v	count
ober,m,oberow	work
obery,v	work
ogas	near
ola,v	weep
oll	all
omlowenhe	enjoy
omma	here
omweles,v	visit
omwolghy,v	wash (oneself)
on,m,en,enas	lamb
onen	one (standing alone)
onyonen,f,onyon	onion
orth	at,by
os,m	age (era)
ottena	there is (demonst.)
otomma	here is (demonst.)
ow^4	-ing
ow^3	my
own,m	fear
owr,m,owrys	hour
owraval,m,owravallow	orange
oy,m,oyow	egg
p'ur ?	what time ? when ?
padel dorn,f,padellow dorn	saucepan
padel,f,padellow	dish,pan
padellyk,m,padellygow	saucer
palas,v	dig
pan^2 ?	when ?
paper,m,paperyow	paper
par,m/f,parow	kind,equal
park-kerry,m,parcow-kerry	car-park

parth,f,parthow	behalf,side
parys,adj	ready
Pask,m	Easter
passa,v	cough
pasty,m,pastys	pasty
patata,m	potato
pe,v	pay
peder,f	four
pel,f,pelyow	ball
peldros,f	football
peldros rugby	rugby
pell,adj	far
pellgewsel,v	phone
pellgowser,m,pellgowserow	phone
pellwolok,f	television (media)
pen,m,pennow	head
penbloth,m	birthday
pendra,f,pendrevow	village (hamlet)
penseythen,f,penseythennow	weekend
perfyth,adj	perfect
peryl,m	danger
peryllys,adj	dangerous
pes	how many
peswar,m	four
peswardhek,adj	fourteen
pesya,v	continue,last
pew,v	own
plans,m,plansow	plant
plat,m,platyow	plate
ple ?	where ?
plos,adj	dirty
plu,f,pluyow	parish
pluven,f,pluvennow	pen
pluven blom,f	pencil
po	or
pobas,v	bake
pobel,f,poblow	people

podyk,m,podygow	jug
poket,m,pokettys	pocket
pol,m,pollow	pool
pons,m,ponsow	bridge
ponya,v	run
popet,m	doll
poran	exactly
pors,m,porsow	purse
porth,m,porthow	harbour,entrance
pos,m,posow	weight
pos,adj	heavy
pot-te,m,pottow-te	teapot
potya,v	kick
pow,m,powyow	country
pow Saws,m	England
pows,f,powsyow	coat
prak ?	why ?
pras,m,prasow	meadow
predery,v	think
prena,v	buy
prenassa,v	shopping (go)
pronter,m,prontoryon	vicar
pry,m	clay
pryas	married
pryntya,v	print
prys,m,prysyow	time (occasion)
prys,m,prysyow	price,worth
prys-bos,m,prysyow-bos	meal
puber,m	pepper
puns,m,punsow	pound
pup	all
pup den oll	everybody
pupla	everywhere
pur,adj	very
py ?	what,who ?
py lyes ?	how much ?
py par ?	what kind of ?

pyben,f	pipe (smoking)
pygemmys ?	how much ?
pymp,adj	five
pymthek,adj	fifteen
pynak	whoever
pynta,m,pyntys	pint
pynyl	which (one)
pys da	pleased
pysen,f,pys	pea
pysk,m,puskes	fish
pysy,v	beg
pyth,m,pythow	thing
pyth ?	what ?
pyu ?	who ?
quarter,m,quartrys	quarter
rak	for
ran,f,rannow	part
re^2	too
re	some
redya,v	read
reken,m	bill (account)
reknel,f,reknellow	calculator
res,m	necessity
resek,v	run
rew,m	ice
rewer,m,reweryow	deep freeze
rewy,v	freeze
ro,m,rohow	present,gift
ros,f,rosow	wheel,net
ruth,f,ruthow	crowd
ruth,adj	red
ry,v	give
ryp	beside
ryth	free (not:cost-free)
Sadorn,m	Saturday

safron,m	saffron
sagh,m,seghyer	bag
saw	except
Saws,m,Sawson	Englishman
Sawses,f,Sawsesow	Englishwoman
Sawsnek	English
scaf,adj	quick
scath,f,scathow	boat
scol,f,scolyow	school
scon,adj	quick
scoth,f,scodhow,dywscoth	shoulder
scovarn,f,dywscovarn	ear
scryfa,v	write
scryja,v	scream
scryvynyades,f,scryvynyadesow	secretary
scryvynyas,m,scryvynysy	secretary
scubel,f,scubellow	brush
scullya,v	waste,spill
seban,m	soap
segh,adj	dry
seghes,m	thirst
selsygen,f,selsyk	sausage
seny,v	ring,sound
serrys	angry
sesya,v	seize
sethyk,m,sethygow	dart
sevel,v	stand
sewya,v	follow
seytek	seventeen
seyth,adj	seven
skentel,adj	wise
skyans,m,skyansow	knowledge
skyber,f,skyberyow	barn
snell,adj	fast,quick
solabrys	formerly
son,m,sonyow	sound
soper,m,soperow	supper

sos	friends
soth,f,sodhow	job
sothva,f,sodhvaow	office
sothva post,f,sothva post	post office
spena,v	spend
splan,adj	shining,splendid,bright
sport,m,sportys	sport
spycer,m,spycers	grocer
spysty,m,spystyow	grocer's shop
squattya,v	hit
squyth,adj	tired
sten,m	tin
stenor,m,stenoryon	miner (tin)
steren,f,col. ster,sterennow	star
stevel,f,stevelyow	room
stevel dybry,f,stevelyow dybry	dining room
stevel omwolghy,f	bathroom
stret,m,stretys	street
strewy,v	sneeze
studhya,v	study
styr,m,styryow	meaning
sugra,m	sugar
Sul	Sunday
sur	sure
sylwel,v	save
synsy,v	hold
syvyen,f,syvy	strawberry
tam,m,tymmyn	bit
tan,m,tanow	fire
tanbren,m,tanbrenyer	match (for striking)
taran,f	thunder
tas,m,tasow	father
tasgwyn,m,tasowgwyn	grandfather
tava,v	touch
tavas,m,tavosow	tongue
te,m	tea

tek,adj	pretty,beautiful
tenewan,m,tenwennow	side
tenna,v	pull
tergwyth	three times
termyn,m,termynyow	term,time
terry,v	break
tesen,f,tesennow	cake
tesen gales,f,tesennow cales	biscuit
tevy,v	grow
tevysak,m,tevysogyon	adult
tevysoges,f,tevysogesow	adult
tew,adj	fat
tewas,col	sand
tewel,v	quiet (be)
tewl,adj	dark
tewlel,v	throw
to,m,tohow	roof
tokyn,m,toknys	ticket
toll,m,tell	hole
tom,adj	hot
ton,m,tonnow	wave (sea)
torth,f,torthow	loaf
tour,m,tourow	tower
towal,m,towellow	towel
towl,m,towlow	plan
towlen,m,towlennow	programme
tra,an dra,taclow	thing
tramor,adj	foreign,overseas
travyth	anything
trawythyow	sometimes
tre,f,trevow	town
tredan,m	electricity
tredanek,adj	electric
tredhek,adj	thirteen
treghy,v	cut
trelya,v	change,turn
tremena,v	pass

tren,trenys	train
trenk,adj	sour
tressa,adj	third
treth,m,trethow	beach
trevas,f,trevasow	harvest,crop
tro,f,troyow	turn,walk
troha	towards
tron,m,tronow	nose
tros,m,treys,deudros	foot
try³,m	three
tryga,v	live,dwell
trygva,f,trygvaow	address
tryst,adj	sad
tu,m,tuyow	direction,side
tus (see den)	men
ty	you (singular)
tyak,m,tyogyon	farmer
tyby,v	think
tylda,m,tyldys	tent
tyller,m,tylleryow	place
tylly,v	owe
tylu,m,tyluyow	family
tyr,m,tyryow	land
tyr³,f	three
ufern,m,deuufern	ankle
ugans,adj	twenty
ughel	high
un,adj	one (with noun)
unnek,adj	eleven
unwyth	once
ur,f,uryow	hour
uryor,m	watch (timepiece)
uskys,adj	quick
uthek,adj	horrible
vyaja,v	travel

war[2]	on
war,adj	careful
warbarth	together
wardhelergh	back,backwards
warlergh	behind,after
whare	soon
wharfos,v	happen
whath	even,still
whegh,adj	six
wheghow	sweets
whel,m,whelyow	mine (with the name)
wherow,adj	bitter
wherthyn,v	laugh
whetek,adj	sixteen
Whevrer,m	February
whor,f,wheryth	sister
why	you
whylas,v	look for
wosa	after
y[2]	him
y[2],m	his,its
y	they
y[5]	verbal particle
yagh,adj	healthy
yar,f,yer	chicken,hen
ydhyn (see edhen),f	birds
yeghes,m	health
yet,f,yettys	gate
yeth,f,yethow	language
yeyn,adj	cold
yeyner,m	refrigerator
ygery,v	open
ylow,m	music
yn	in
yn ban	upstairs

yn chy	home (at)
yn kever	about
yn mes	out
yn meth	says,said
yn mysk	among
yn nans	down
yn tyen	completely
yn-[5]	-ly before adj
ynban	up
yndan	beneath,under
yndella,adv	thus,so
yndella,adj	so
ynter	between
ynter	among
yntra	among
ynweth	also
yowynk,adj	young
ys	lower (prefix)
ysel	low
yskynna,v	climb up,reach
yth[5]	verbal particle
ytho	so,therefore
Ywerdhon,f	Ireland

about	yn kever
above	a ugh, awartha
accident	droklam, m, droklammow
account	acont, m
accuracy	kewerder, m
accurate	kewar, adj
across	a drus
address	trygva, f, trygvaow
adult (woman)	tevysoges, f, tevysogesow
adult (man)	tevysak, m, tevysogyon
aeroplane	ayren, f, ayrennow
after	wosa
afternoon	dohajeth
again	arta
against	erbyn
age (years old)	bloth, m
age (era)	os, m
agriculture	ameth, f
alive	bew
all	oll, pup
almost	namna^2
along	ahes
also	ynweth, kekefrys
although	kyn^5
ambulance	clafcar, m, clafkerry
among	yntra, ynter, yn mysk
and	ha, hag
angry	serrys
animal	myl, m, mylas
	eneval, m, enevelas
ankle	ufern, m, deuufern
another	aral
answer	gorthyp, m
anything	travyth
appetite	ewl bos, f
apple	aval, m, avallow
approach	nessa, v

April	mys Ebrel,m
apron	apern,m,apronyow
arm	bregh,f,dywvregh
armchair	cadar vreghek,f,caderyow breghek
around	adro
arrive	dos,v
as	del
as much	kemmys
as soon as	kettel
ashes	lusow,f
ask	govyn,v
at night	noswyth
at	orth
August	mys Est,m
aunt	modryp,f,modrebeth
autumn	Kynyaf,m
baby	baban,m/f,babanas
back (of body)	keyn,m,keynow
back,backwards	wardhelergh
bacon	bakken,m
bad	drok,adj
bag	sagh,m,seghyer
bake	pobas,v
ball	pel,f,pelyow
bank	arghanty,m,arghantyow
bard (female)	bardhes,f,bardhesow
bard (male)	barth,m,byrth
bark	hartha,v
barn	skyber,f,skyberyow
basin	bason,m,basonnow
basket	canstel,f,canstellow
bat (cricket)	bat,m,battys
bathe	badhya,v
bathroom	stevel omwolghy,f
be	bos,v
be able	gallos,v
beach	treth,m,trethow

bean	faven,f,faf
beard	barf,f,barvow
beat	fetha,v
beautiful	tek,adj
because	awos
bed	gwely,m,gwelyow
bedroom	chambour,m,chambours
beef	kyk bowyn,m
beer	coref,m
before	kens
beg	pysy,v
begin	dalleth,v
behalf	parth,f,parthow
behind	adryf dhe,adhelergh
believe	crysy,v
below	awoles
beneath	yndan
beside	ryp
best	gwella,adj
better	gwell,adj
between	ynter
bicycle	dywros,f,dywrosow
big	bras
bill (account)	reken,m
bird	edhen,f,ydhyn
birthday	penbloth,m
biscuit	tesen gales,f,tesennow cales
bit	tam,m,tymmyn
bit (small piece)	darn,m,darnow
bite,chew	dynsel,v
bitter	wherow,adj
black	du,adj
blackberry	moren,f,mor
blind	dall,adj
blood	gos,m
blue	glas,adj
boat	scath,f,scathow
body	corf,m,corfow

bone	ascorn,m,eskern
book	lyver,m,lyfrow
born	genys
bottle	bottel,m,bottellow
bowl	bolla,m,bollow
box	kyst,f,kystyow
boy	maw,m,mebyon
bread	bara,m
break	terry,v
breakfast	hansel,m,hansellow
Breton (female)	Bretones,f,Bretonyon
Breton (male)	Breton,m,Bretonyon
bridge	pons,m,ponsow
bright	splan,adj
bring	dry,v
Britain	Breten vur,f
British	Bretennek
Brittany	Breten vyghan,f
brother	broder,m,breder
brown	gell,adj
brush	scubel,f,scubellow
bucket	kelorn,m
build	drehevel,v
bump	bonk,m,bonkys
bundle,luggage	fardel,m,fardellow
burn	lesky,v
bus	kyttryn,m,kyttrynyow
	bus,m,bussow
bus-stop	busaf,m,busavow
bush	bos,m
business	negys,m,negysyow
busy	bysy
but	mes
butcher	kyger,m
butter	amanyn,m
buy	prena,v
by	orth

cabbage	cawlen,f,cawl
cake	tesen,f,tesennow
calculator	reknel,f,reknellow
call (invite,name)	gelwel,v
can (tin)	cafas,m,cafasow
car	car,m,kerry
car-park	park-kerry,m,parcow-kerry
card	carten,f,cartennow
careful	war,adj
carrot	caretysen,f,caretys
carry	don,v
cat	cath,f,cathas
cattle	gwarthek,col
ceiling	nen,m,nennow
cement	keskelm,m
cemetery	enclathva,f
centre (circle)	cres,m
centre (health...)	cresen,f
certain	dyogel,adj
chair	cadar,f,caderyow
chairman	caderyer,m,caderyoryon
change	trelya,v
cheap	a brys ysel
cheek	bogh,f,dywvogh
cheese	kes,m
chew	dynsel,v
chicken	yar,f,yer
child	flogh,m,fleghes
chimney	chymbla,m
chin	elgeth,f,elgethyow
chip	asclejen,f,asclas
chips	asclas,col
chipshop	asclatty,m,asclattyow
choose	dewys,v
Christmas	Nadelek,m
church	eglos,f,eglosyow
cider	cyder,m

cigarette	cygaret,m,cygaretys
claw	ewyn,m,ewynas
clay	pry,m
clean	glan,adj
clean	glanhe,v
clever	connek,adj
cliff	als,f,alsyow
climb up	yskynna,v
clock	clok,m
close	degea,v
closer	nes
cloth	len,f,lennow
clothes	dyllajow
cloud	comolen,f,comol
coal (fuel)	glow,col
coat	pows,f,powsyow
coffee	coffy,m
coin	bath,m,bathow
cold	anwos,m
cold	yeyn,adj
colour	lyw,m,lywyow
comb	cryb,f,crybow
come	dos,v
come down	dyeskynna,v
completely	yn tyen
computer	kempoller,m
concrete	kentevyn,m
continue	pesya,v
cook	kegy,v
cooker	coger,m,cogeryow
corner	elyn,m,elynnow
Cornish	Kernewek,adj
Cornishman	Kernow,m,Kernowyon
Cornishwoman	Kernewes,f,Kernewesow
Cornwall	Kernow,f
correct	ewn,adj
correct	ewna,v
cost	cost,m,costys

cough	passa,v
council	consel,m
councillor	consler,m
count	nyvera,v
country	pow,m,powyow
	gwlas,f,gwlasow
	bro,f,broyow
cousin (male)	kenderow,m,kendrywy
cousin (female)	kenytherow,f,kenythrywy
cow	bugh,f,bughas
crab	canker,m,kencras
cream	dehen,m
crisp (potato)	cresyk,cresygow
crop	trevas,f,trevasow
crossroads	crowshensy
crow	bran,f,bryny
crowd	bush,m,bushys
crumb	brewyonen,brewyon
cry	crya,v
cup	hanaf,m,hanavow
cupboard	amary,m,amarys
curse	mollethy,v
curtain	croglen,f
cut	treghy,v
dance	donsya,v
danger	peryl,m
dangerous	peryllys,adj
dare	bedha,v
dark	tewl,adj
dart	sethyk,m,sethygow
daughter	myrgh,f,myrghes
day	deth,m,dedhyow
day before yesterday	degensete,m
dead	marow,adj
deaf	bodhar,adj
dear	cuf,adj
dear	ker

December	mys Kevardhu,m
decide	ervyra,v
deep	down,adj
deep freeze	rewer,m,reweryow
dentist	dynsor,m,dynsoryon
deny	nagha,v
destroy	dystrewy,v
devil	jawl,m
Devon	Dewnans,f
dictionary	gerlyver,m,gerlyfrow
die	merwel,v
difficult	cales
dig	palas,v
dining room	stevel dybry,f,stevelyow dybry
dinner (midday)	kynyow,m,kynyewyow
direction,side	tu,m,tuyow
dirty	plos,adj
dish	padel,f,padellow
do	gul,v
doctor (male)	medhek,m,medhygyon
doctor (female)	medheges,f,medhegesow
dog	ky,m,cun
doll	popet,m
door	darras,m,darrajow
down	yn nans
draw	delynya,v
dream	hunros,m
dress	gwysca,v
drink	dewas,f,dewosow
drink	eva,v
drive (a car)	lewyas,v
drop	bera,v
drown	budhy,v
drunk	medhow,adj
dry	segh,adj
duck	hos,m,heyjy
dust	dowst,m
dustbin	atalgyst,f,atalgystyow

dwell (live)	tryga,v
ear	scovarn,f,dywscovarn
early	avar
earn	dyndyl,v
east	howldrehevel,m
Easter	Pask,m
easy	es,adj
eat	dybry,v
edge	amal,m,emlow
egg	oy,m,oyow
eight	eth,adj
eighteen	etek,adj
elbow	elyn,m,deuelyn
electric	tredanek,adj
electricity	tredan,m
eleven	unnek,adj
empty	gwak,adj
end	dewedha,v
end	deweth,m
England	pow Saws,m
English	Sawsnek
Englishman	Saws,m,Sawson
Englishwoman	Sawses,f,Sawsesow
enjoy	omlowenhe
enough	lowr,adj
enter	entra,v
envelope	maylyer,m
equal	par
even	whath
evening	gorthewer,m
ever	byth,bythqueth
everybody	pup den oll
everywhere	pupla
exactly	poran
example	ensompel,m,ensomplys
except	saw
eye	lagas,m,deulagas

face	enep,m,enebow
factory	gwythva,f
fail	fyllel,v
fair	whek,adj
fall	codha,v
family	tylu,m,tyluyow
far	pell,adj
farm	bargen tyr,m
farmer	tyak,m,tyogyon
fast	snell,adj
fat	tew,adj
father	tas,m,tasow
fear	own,m
February	mys Whevrer,m
fetch	kerghes ,v
few	nebes
field (large,open)	mes,m,mesyow
fifteen	pymthek,adj
fill	lenwel,v
find	cafos,v
fine (splendid)	braf,adj
finger	bys,m,besyas
fingernail	ewyn,m,ewynas
finish	gorfenna,v
fire	tan,m,tanow
first	kensa
fish	pysk,m,puskes
fishing boat	cok,m,cucow
fist	dorn,m,deudhorn
five	pymp,adj
flag	baner,m,banerow
floor (ground)	lur,m,luryow
flour	bles,m
flower	blejen,f,blejennow
fly	nyja,v
fog	newl,m
follow	sewya,v

food	bos,m
foolish	fol,adj
foot	tros,m,treys,deudros
football	peldros,f
for	rak
for ever	bys vyken
for (on the part of)	abarth
foreign	tramor,adj
forget	ankevy,v
forgive	gava,v
fork	forgh,f,fergh
formerly	solabrys
four	peswar,m
four	peder,f
fourteen	peswardhek,adj
France	pow Frynk,f
free (not:cost-free)	ryth
free (without cost)	hep cost
freeze	rewy,v
fresh	er,adj
Friday	de Gwener
friend (male)	car,m,kerens
friend (female)	coweth,m,cowetha
friends	sos
	kerens,m
from	dyworth,adhyworth
	a^2
fruit	frut,m,frutys
fry	frya,v
full	lun,adj
furniture	mebyl,col
game	gwary,m
garage	carjy,m,carjyow
garden	lowarth,f,lowarthow
gate	yet,f,yettys
get	cafos,v
gift	ro,m,rohow

girl	mowes,f,mowysy
give	ry,v
glass (drinking)	gwedren,f,gwedrennow
glass (material)	gweder,m,gwedrow
glove	manek,f,manegow
glue	glus,m
go	mos,v
goat	gavar,f,gever
God	Dew
good	da,adj
goodbye	Dew genes
grandchild	floghwyn,m,fleghes gwyn
grandfather	tasgwyn,m,tasowgwyn
granny	damawyn,f,dammyow gwyn
grave	beth,m,bedhow
great	mur,adj
green	gwer,adj
grey	los,adj
grief	galar,m
grocer	spycer,m,spycers
grocer's shop	spysty,m,spystyow
ground	lur,f,luryow
group	bagas,m,bagasow
grow	tevy,v
guess	desmygy,v
gun	gon,m,gonnys
hair	blewen,f,blew
half	hanter
hall	hel,m,helow
hammer	morthol,m,mortholow
hand	luf,f,dywluf
hand	dorn,m,deudhorn
hang	cregy,v
happen	wharfos,v
happy	lowen,adj
harbour	porth,m,porthow
hard	cales

harvest	trevas,f,trevasow
hat	hot,m
hateful	cas,adj
have	cafos,v
he	ef
head	pen,m,pennow
health	yeghes,m
healthy	yagh,adj
hear	clewes,v
heavy	pos,adj
hedge	ke,m,keow
help	gweres,v
hen	yar,f,yer
her	hy,f
here	omma
here is (demonst.)	otomma
hide	cudha,v
high	ughel
hill	meneth,m,menythyow
	bre,f,breow
	bryn,m,brynnow
him	y^2
his	y^2,m
hit	squattya,v
hold	synsy,v
hole	toll,m,tell
holiday	degol,m,degolyow
home (at)	yn chy
honey	mel,m
hope	gwaytya,v
horrible	uthek,adj
horse	margh,m,mergh
hospital	clavjy,m,clavjyow
hot	tom,adj
hour	owr,m,owrys
	ur,f,uryow
house	chy,m,chyow
how	fatel

how many	pes
how much ?	pygemmys ?
	py lyes ?
hundred	cans,m,cansow
hunger	nown,m
hurry	fystyna,v
husband	gour,m
ice	rew,m
ice cream	dehen rewys,m
if	mar^4
ill	claf,adj
immediately	dystough
improve	gwellhe,v
in	yn
in front of	arak
	adherak
inch	mesva,f,mesvedhy
industry	dywysygneth,m
-ing	ow^4
invent	desmygy,v
invite	gelwel,v
Ireland	Ywerdhon,f
island	enys,f,enesow
it (m)	ef
it	hy,f
item of clothing	dyllas,m,dyllajow
jam	kyfyth,m
January	mys Genver,m
job	soth,f,sodhow
join	junnya,v
jug	podyk,m,podygow
July	mys Gortheren,m
jump	lamma,v
June	mys Metheven,m

kettle	caltor,f,caltoryow
key	alwheth,m,alwhethow
kick	potya,v
kill	ladha,v
kind	cuf,adj
kind (sort)	par
king	myghtern,m,myghterneth
kitchen	kegyn,f,kegynow
knee	glyn,m,deulyn
knife	collel,f,kellyl
know (recognise)	aswon,v
know (understand)	gothvos,v
knowledge	skyans,m,skyansow
lake	lyn,f,lynnow
lamb	on,m,en,enas
lame	cloppek,adj
land	tyr,m,tyryow
lane	bownder,f,bownderyow
language	yeth,f,yethow
last	pesya,v
late	dewedhes
laugh	wherthyn,v
lavatory	chy byghan,m,chyow byghan
law	lagha,m,laghys
lazy	dyek,adj
lead	hembronk,v
leaf	delen,f,del,delkyow
learn	dysky,v
least	lyha
leave	gasa,v
left	cleth,adj
leg	gar,f,dywar
lend	cola orth,v
length	hes,m
less	le
lesson	dyscas,m,dyscasow
letter	lyther,m,lytheryow

library (building)	lyverjy,m,lyverjyow
library (of books)	lyverva,f
lid	gorher,m,gorheryow
lie down	growetha,v
life	bewnans,m,bewnansow
lift	drehevel,v
light	golow,m,golowys
lightning	lughes,col
like	hevelep
	avel
	kepar
listen	goslowes,v
live,dwell	tryga,v
lively	bew
loaf	torth,f,torthow
London	Loundres,f
long	hyr,adj
look at	myras orth,v
look for	whylas,v
lorry	kert,m,kertys
lose	kelly,v
love	cara,v
low	ysel
lower (prefix)	ys
lucky	fusyk,adj
luggage	fardel,m,fardellow
lunch (picnic)	crowst,m,crowstys
-ly	yn^5
make	gul,v
man	den,m,tus
many	lyes,adj
map	mappa,m,mappys
March	mys Merth,m
market	marghas,f,marghasow
married	pryas
match (for striking)	tanbren,m,tanbrenyer
match (game)	fyt,m,fyttys

May	mys Me,m
meadow	pras,m,prasow
meal	prys-bos,m,prysyow-bos
meaning	styr,m,styryow
meat	kyk,m
medicine	medhekneth,m
men	tus (see den)
mend	ewna,v
message	negys,m,negysyow
middle	cres,m,cresow
mile	myldyr,m,myldyryow
milk	leth,m
mill	melyn,f,melynyow
mine	bal,m,balow
mine (with the name)	whel,m,whelyow
miner (tin)	stenor,m,stenoryon
minute	mynysen,f,mynysennow
mirror	gweder myras,m
mixture	kemysk,m
Monday	de Lun
money	arghans
month	mys,m,mysyow
moon	lor,f
more	moy
morning	myttyn,m,myttynow
most	moyha
mother	mam,f,mammow
mouth	ganow,m,ganowow
move	gwaya,v
music	ylow,m
my	ow[3]
name	gelwel,v
name	hanow,m,hynwyn
narrow	cul,adj
nation	kenethel,f,kenethlow
near	ogas
nearest	nessa

necessity	res,m
neck	conna,m
need	ethom,m
nephew	noy,m,noyens
nest	nyth,m
net	ros,f
never	nefra
new	noweth,adj
news	newodhow
next	nessa
night	nos,f,nosow
night (last night)	nyhewer
nine	naw
nineteen	nawnjek
no more	namoy
nor	na,nag
north	cleth
nose	tron,m,tronow
not	ny^2
	na,nag
November	mys Du,m
now	lemmyn
number	nyver,m,nyverow
nurse	clavyjores,f,clavyjoresow
October	mys Hedra,m
of	a ν
office	sothva,f,sodhvaow
often	menough
old	hen,coth,adj
on	war^2
on time	adermyn
once	unwyth
one (standing alone)	onen
one (with noun)	un,adj
onion	onyonen,f,onyon
open	ygery,v
opposite	adal

or	po
orange	owraval,m,owravallow
order	gorhemmyn,erghy,v
other,others	aral,erel
our	agan
out	mes,yn mes
outside	aves
oven	forn,f,fornow
over	dres
overseas	tramor,adj
owe	tylly,v
own	pew,v
page	folen,f,folennow
pain	galar,m
pan	padel,f,padellow
paper	paper,m,paperyow
parents	kerens,m
parish	plu,f,pluyow
part	ran,f,rannow
party (birthday..)	kyfvewy,m
pass	tremena,v
past	dres
pay	gober,m,gobrow
pay	pe,v
pea	pysen,f,pys
pen	pluven,f,pluvennow
pencil	pluven blom,f
penny	deneren,f,denerennow
people	pobel,f,poblow
pepper	puber,m
perfect	perfyth,adj
perhaps	martesen
phone	pellgewsel,v
phone	pellgowser,m,pellgowserow
picture	lywyans,m,lywyansow
pig	hogh,m,mogh
pint	pynta,m,pyntys

pipe (smoking)	pyben,f
place	tyller,m,tylleryow
	le,m,leow
plan	towl,m,towlow
plant	plans,m,plansow
plate	plat,m,platyow
play	gwary,v
play an instrument	cana,v
please	mar plek
pleased	pys da
pocket	poket,m,pokettys
policeman	gwythyas,m,gwythysy
policewoman	gwythyades,f,gwythyadesow
pool	pol,m,pollow
poor	boghosek,adj
pork	kyk mogh,m
post office	sothva post,f,sothva post
post-card	carten-post,f,cartennow-p.
postman	lytherwas,m,lytherwesyon
potato	patata,m
pound	puns,m,punsow
pour	devera,v
powerful	gallosek,adj
present (gift)	ro,m,rohow
pretty	tek,adj
price	prys,m,prysyow
print	pryntya,v
programme	towlen,m,towlennow
promise	ambosa,dedhewy,v
pub	dewotty,m,dewottyow
pull	tenna,v
purse	pors,m,porsow
put	gorra,v
quarter	quarter,m,quartrys
queen	myghternes,f,myghternesow
question	govyn,m
quick	uskys,snell,scon,scaf,adj

quiet	cosel,adj
quiet (be)	tewel,v
rabbit	conyn,m,conynas
railway	forth-horn,f,fordhow-horn
rain	glaw,m
reach	ystynna,v
read	redya,v
ready	parys,adj
recently	degensow,agensow
red	ruth,adj
refrigerator	yeyner,m
refuse	nagha,v
regret	edrek,m
remember	cofhe,v
reply	gortheby,v
restaurant	bosty,m,bostyow
return	dewheles,v
right	dyghow,m
ring	bysow,m,besewow
ring	seny,v
ripe	athves
river	avon,f,avenow
road	forth,f,fordhow
rock	carrek,f,carrygy
roof	to,m,tohow
room	stevel,f,stevelyow
rope	lovan,f,lovonnow
rough	garow,adj
round	cren,adj
rubbish (verbal)	flows,m
run	ponya,resek,v
sad	tryst,adj
safe	dyogel,adj
said	yn meth
sailor	marner,m,marners
sale	gwerth,f

salt	holan,m
same	keth
sand	tewas,col
Saturday	de Sadorn
saucepan	padel dorn,f,padellow dorn
saucer	padellyk,m,padellygow
sausage	selsygen,f,selsyk
save	sylwel,v
say	leverel,v
says,said	yn meth
school	scol,f,scolyow
scissors	gwelsow byghan,m
Scotland	Alban,f
scream	scryja,v
sea	mor,m,morow
seat	eseth,f,esedhow
secretary (male)	scryvynyas,m,scryvynysy
secretary (female)	scryvynyades,f,scryvynyadesow
see	gweles,v
seize	sesya,v
self	honen
sell	gwertha,v
send	danvon,v
September	mys Gwyngala,m
seven	seyth,adj
seventeen	seytek
shake	crenna,v
shame	meth,f
shape	furf,f,furvyow
share	kevranna,v
sharp	lym,adj
she	hy,f
shed	crow,m,crowyow
sheep	davas,f,deves
shelf	estyllen,f,estyllenow
shining	splan,adj
ship	gorhel,m,gorholyon
shirt	crys,m,crysyow

shoe	eskys,f,skyjyow
shop	gwerthjy,m,gwerthjyow
shopping (to go..)	prenassa,v
short	ber,adj
shoulder	scoth,f,scodhow,dywscoth
shout	garma,v
show	dysquedhes,v
shut	degea,v
sick	claf,adj
side	tenewan,m,tenwennow
side (on behalf)	parth,f,parthow
side (direction)	tu,m,tuyow
side (edge)	amal,m,emlow
sing	cana,v
sister	whor,f,wheryth
sit	esedha,v
sitting-room	esethva,f,esethvaow
six	whegh,adj
sixteen	whelek,adj
skin	croghen,f
skirt	losten,f,lostennow
sky	ebren,f
sleep	cusca,v
slim	mon,adj
slope	leder,f,ledrow
slow	lent,adj
small	byghan
smell	blas,m
smell	clewes,v
smoke	megy,v
sneeze	strewy,v
snow	ergh,m
so	mar²
so	yndella,adj
so that	may,mayth⁵
so (therefore)	ytho
soap	seban,m
society	cowethas,f,cowethasow

soft	medhel,adj
some	re,nebes
someone	nebonen
something	neppyth
sometimes	trawythyow
son	map,m,mebyon
song	can,f,cannow
soon	whare
sound	son,m,sonyow
sound	seny,v
soup	cowl,m
sour	trenk,adj
south	dyghow,m
speak	kewsel,v
spend	spena,v
spill	sculya,v
splendid	splan,adj
splendid	braf
spoon	lo,f,loyow
sport	sport,m,sportys
spring	Gwaynten,v
squeeze	gwasca,v
stairs	grysys
stand	sevel,v
star	steren,f,ster,sterennow,col
start	dalleth,m
station	gorsaf,m,gorsavow
steal	ladra,v
step	cam,m,cammow
stick	glena orth,v
still	whath
stone	men,m,meyn
stop	hedhy,v
storm	hager awel,f
strange	coynt,adj
stranger	estren,m,estrenyon
strawberry	syvyen,f,syvy
street	stret,m,stretys

strength	nerth,m
strong	cref,adj
study	studhya,v
stupid	goky,adj
sudden	desempys,adj
suddenly	adhesempys
sugar	sugra,m
summer	Haf,m,Havow
sun	howl,m
Sunday	de Sul
supper	con,f
	soper,m,soperow
sure	sur
surprise	marth,m
swallow	collenky,lenky,v
swear	mollethy,v
sweet	whek,adj
sweets	whegow
swim	nuvya,v
table	mos,f,mosow
tail	lost,m,lostow
take	kemeres,v
talk	kewsel,v
taste	blas,m
tea	te,m
teacher (male)	dyscajor,m,dyscajoryon
teacher (female)	dyscajores,f,dyscajoresow
team	bagas,m,bagasow
teapot	pot-te,m,pottow-te
television	pellwolok,f
tell	leverel,deryvas,v
ten	dek
tent	tylda,m,tyldys
term	termyn,m,termynyow
than	es,ages
thanks	mur ras

that	hen,m
	hon,f
	-na
that (that one)	henna,m
	honna,f
that (so that)	may,mayth[5]
the	an
their	aga
there	ena
there is (demonst.)	ottena
therefore	ytho
they	y
thief	lader,m,ladron
thing	pyth,m,pythow
	tra,taclow
think	tyby,predery,v
third	tressa,adj
thirst	seghes,m
thirteen	tredhek,adj
this	-ma
	hem,m
	hom,f
this (this one)	hemma,m
	homma,f
thousand	myl,f,mylyow
three	try[3],m
	tyr[3],f
three times	tergwyth
through	dre[2]
throw	tewlel,v
thunder	taran,f
Thursday	de Yow
thus	yndella,adv
ticket	tokyn,m,toknys
tidy	kempen,adj
tie	kelmy,v
time	amser,f,amserow
time (occasion)	prys,m,prysyow

time (term)	termyn,m,termynyow
tin (metal)	sten,m
tired	squyth,adj
to	dhe²
toast	cras,col
today	hedhyu
together	warbarth
tomorrow	avorow
tongue	tavas,m,tavosow
tonight	haneth
too	re²
tooth	dans,m,dyns
top	gwartha,m
touch	tava,v
towards	troha
towel	towal,m,towellow
tower	tour,m,tourow
town	tre,f,trevow
train	tren,trenys
travel	vyaja,v
tree	gwedhen,f,gwyth
trousers	lavrak,m,lavregow
true	gwyr,adj
try	assaya,v
Tuesday	de Merth
turn	trelya,v
turn	tro,f,troyow
twelve	deudhek
twenty	ugans,adj
twice	dywwyth
two	deu²,m
	dyw²,f
ugly	hager,adj
uncle	ewnter,m,ewntras
under	yndan
understand	gothvos,convedhes,v
unless	marnas

until	erna², bys
up	ynban
upstairs	yn ban
useful	dhe les, adj
valley	nans, m, nansow
valley (dry)	glyn, m, glynnow
vegetable	losowen, f, losow
-verbal particles-	a²
	yth, y⁵
very	pur, adj
vicar	pronter, m, prontoryon
village (hamlet)	pendra, f, pendrevow
visit	omweles, v
voice	lef, m, levow
wait	gortos, v
wake up	dyfuna, v
Wales	Kembry
walk	kerdhes, v
walk	tro, f, troyow
wall	fos, f, fosow
wander	gwandra, v
want	mynnes, v
war	bresel, m/f, breselow
wash (not oneself)	golghy, v
wash (oneself)	omwolghy, v
waste	scullya, v
watch (timepiece)	uryor, m
water	dowr, m, dowrow
wave (sea)	ton, m, tonnow
way	forth, f, fordhow
we	ny
weak	gwan, adj
wear	gwysca, v
weather	kewer, f
wedding	demedhyans, m, demedhyansow
Wednesday	de Mergher

weekend	penseythen,f,penseythennow
weep	ola,v
weight	pos,m,posow
well	fenten,f,fentynyow
Welsh	Kembrek
Welshman	Kembro,m,Kembryon
Welshwoman	Kembres,f,Kembresow
west	howlsedhas,m
wet	glyp,adj
what ?	pyth ?
what kind of ?	py par ?
what time ?	p'ur ?
what ?	py ?
wheel	ros,f,rosow
when	pan[2]
where (relative)	may,mayth[5]
where ?	ple ?
which (one)	pyny1
while	hedra
white	gwyn,adj
who (relative)	nep
who ?	pyu ?
	py ?
whoever	pynak
whole	cowal,adj
why ?	prak ?
wide	efan,ledan,adj
width	les,m
wife	gwrek,f,gwrageth
win	gwaynya,v
wind	gwyns,m,gwynsow
window	fenester,f,fenestry
wine	gwyn,m
wing	askel,f,eskelly
winter	Gwaf,m,Gwavow
wise	fur,skentel,adj
wish	bolunjeth,m
with	gans

without	hep,heb
woman	benen,f,benenes
wonderful	marthys,adj
wool	gwlan,col
word	ger,m,geryow
work	ober,m,oberow
work	obery,v
world	bys,m
	nor,m
worse	gweth,lacca,adj
worst	gwetha,adj
	an lacca
worth	prys,m
write	scryfa,v
wrong	cam,adj
year	bledhen,f,bledhynnow
years	bloth,m
yellow	melen,adj
yesterday	de,m
you (plural)	why
you (singular)	ty
young	yowynk,adj
your (plural)	agas
your (singular)	dha^2
zoo	mylva,f,mylvaow